How to Use This Book

The gospel for each Sunday, as well as Christmas Day, Ash Wednesday, and the Triduum, is listed at the top of the page for that day. You will find the other readings listed there also.

Each week, read the gospel passage before you leave home, or even earlier in the week. Each reflection in this book focuses on a single phrase from the assigned gospel. Use these reflections as part of your preparation and as a way of extending the gospel message throughout the week. The simple question at the end of each reflection provides a springboard for prayer and application.

Some have found that they read in a quiet setting before attending Eucharist. Others tell us that they keep this book in the car and take time waiting in traffic to focus on the phrase or the question for each week, returning to it throughout the week. Still others find that they use these reflections and questions as part of prayer before parish meetings in any given week.

The Word of God is proclaimed in our churches each time we gather for Eucharist. Allowing the gospel to re-sound in our ears and minds and hearts throughout the week will help it take root in our lives.

November 30

First Sunday of Advent

Jerome Kodell, OSB

Lectionary 2B *Isa 63:16b-17, 19b; 64:2-7; Ps 80; 1 Cor 1:3-9*
Mark 13:33-37

"You do not know when the lord of the house is coming."

This passage is the culmination of a short series of sayings and parables about the coming of the Son of Man in glory at the end. In the preceding sections we are told to watch for the signs, but here the message is to be vigilant at all times because, in fact, the signs that are mentioned (disturbance in the heavens) occur periodically, not only once at the end of history.

Watching for the coming of the Son of Man is not something to be worked into the schedule. It is the schedule. So it must become part of what we are doing all the time every day, in other words, living in expectancy of the imminent return of Christ in glory.

According to Cardinal Newman, this is the recipe for becoming a saint. Being holy, he says, is not so much a matter of doing this and not doing that, but having a grace-formed "frame of mind," a main ingredient of which is "living habitually in the light of the world to come." God is coming to us every day, and if we are always alert to welcome him, we will be ready when he comes now and at the end.

A Year of Sundays

Gospel Reflections 2009

Dan Borlik, CM
Mary J. Glynn, SJC
Roy Goetz
John Hall
J. Gaston Hebert
Dan Hennessey
Lilly Hess
Judy Hoelzeman
Rosa María Icaza, CCVI
Jerome Kodell, OSB
David LeSieur
Susan McCarthy, RDC
Robert L. Morris
Marie Morris
Jerre Roberts
Cackie Upchurch
Nancy Lee Walters
Macrina Wiederkehr, OSB
Gregory C. Wolfe
Clifford M. Yeary
Frank Zanoff

Editor: Cackie Upchurch
Associate Editor: Clifford M. Yeary

LITTLE ROCK SCRIPTURE STUDY

A ministry of the Diocese of Little Rock
in partnership with Liturgical Press

Cover design by Ann Blattner.

Little Rock Scripture Study logo originally designed by Maria Estaún; modified by Lisa Walz.

ISSN 1554-6071

ISBN 978-0-8146-3130-0

Introduction

"The eyes of all look hopefully to you;
you give them their food in due season."

(Ps 145:15)

Who hasn't marveled at nature and found in the changing seasons some wisdom from the Creator and Sustainer of all that is good? Many parts of the world experience definite seasons. Winter displays the bare bones of God's creation, stripping the world in a way that makes us anticipate some new life that will no doubt come in with the winds of spring. The green softness of spring gives way to the brilliance of summer light, and in just a few months we ready ourselves for the relief of autumn. As the air cools and leaves fall we slip into a kind of reflective quiet as the earth prepares to make the cycle again.

The church too provides a cycle that can be seen as seasons. We begin in Advent, journey through Christmas, enter into Lent and then Easter. And in between, our year is punctuated by ordered (or ordinary) time. We celebrate great feasts after weeks of preparation. We journey through God's Word by focusing on Old and New Testament readings, and by focusing generally on readings from one central gospel each year.

This particular year is referred to as "Year B," and it focuses on the story of Jesus as found in the Gospel according to Mark. While there will be occasional readings from the other gospels, Mark provides the framework for this year. Beginning in Advent of 2008, and proceeding through the feast of Christ the King at the end of November in 2009, we will encounter Jesus as seen through the lens of Mark and the community to whom he originally wrote.

Allow yourself to enter into the seasons of the church year and to find in them opportunities to feast on the fruits of those seasons. In the order of creation we see that life springs forth, and in the order of the church year, we can expect life to emerge in us as well.

The Lord Jesus will give us food in due season, but we have to come into the fields ready to reap the harvest of his Word whatever the season.

Is Advent a season on my schedule, or a reminder of a year-round way of living in expectation?

December 7

Second Sunday of Advent

Cackie Upchurch

Lectionary 5B
Mark 1:1-8

Isa 40:1-5, 9-11; Ps 85; 2 Pet 3:8-14

John the Baptist appeared in the desert.

In the pages of our Bibles it always seems to be the desert where God is made manifest: Moses encountered God in a burning bush and on a high desert mountain; those enslaved in Egypt passed through waters into a more desolate place before entering Canaan; Jacob camped by a desert spring to prepare himself to reconcile with Esau and in the night had a life-changing encounter with a divine presence. Even Jesus himself went to the desert to pray, and in facing Satan he experienced ministering angels.

In desert areas, every drop of water is essential. For John the Baptist, the Jordan River is God's own meeting place and all who come can be assured of an encounter with the divine. John is merely the servant who invites the guests, washes them clean, and announces the kingdom.

Centuries before John the Baptist, Hosea the prophet spoke God's words about Israel saying, "I will allure her; / I will lead her into the desert / and speak to her heart" (Hos 2:16). Advent is the time when God courts us by inviting us into the desert. It remains a fundamentally perfect place to hear a voice directing us to God's very presence and desires for us.

Where are the streams where I am being invited to encounter God even when life seems dry and barren?

December 14

Third Sunday of Advent

Clifford M. Yeary

Lectionary 8B
John 1:6-8, 19-28

Isa 61:1-2a, 10-11; Luke 1:46f; 1 Thess 5:16-24

"Who are you, so we can give an answer to those who sent us?"

Do any of us really know who we are? Wouldn't that suggest knowing exactly what we were put here to do? John, it seems, was pretty certain of who he wasn't. He also knew that his whole life's mission was about preparing a way for that one for whom everyone should be waiting. If only we could be so certain about our mission in life. Wouldn't it be something to know for sure? And yet John shows us what it is, doesn't he? It's about preparing a way, a way for Jesus to enter our lives.

How does Jesus find a way to reach us? The way to my heart could be a pretty cumbersome journey—lots of rocks and not much of a trail at all. That's why John is such a powerful example. John shouts and the people listen. The time is at hand, get ready for the one who is to come! No dilly-dallying, no lollygagging! And yet John seems to know that all the preparation in the world doesn't bring the one who is to come. He comes of his own will; he comes because he wants to find us. Come, Lord Jesus. We await you in joyful hope.

If someone demanded to know who you were, would your answer send them looking for the Christ?

December 21

Fourth Sunday of Advent

Monsignor J. Gaston Hebert

Lectionary 11B *2 Sam 7:1-5, 8b-12, 14a, 16; Ps 89; Rom 16:25-27*
Luke 1:26-38

"Nothing will be impossible for God."

Don't you just hate it when something upsets your plans? Mary's parents had carefully arranged this wedding. Mary and Joseph had doubtlessly been dreaming of their impending marriage. A visit from an angel changed everything.

We never really know what God has in mind. We can only be sure that it is far more glorious than anything we have planned. "May it be done to me according to your word" tends to stick in the throat when God's plans vary from our own. God often chooses the unexpected as an avenue to enter our lives and to evoke greatness from us that we never knew existed. Our Father wants each of his children to reach his or her potential.

A pregnancy prior to marriage would obviously have been difficult for Mary to explain both to her parents and to Joseph. This wasn't in Mary's plans. Questions are asked of the angel, answers given and accepted. Mary's plans changed in her humble acceptance of God's will rather than her own. She had no way of knowing how this humble flexibility would affect salvation history.

Challenges, crosses, problems will come to us all. They may well be gifts from God to enable us to achieve the greatness he always envisioned for us.

When have I recognized God equipping me for a task or situation that would normally be beyond my capacity or outside of my plans?

December 25

Nativity of the Lord

Judy Hoelzeman

Lectionary 15ABC
Luke 2:15-20

Isa 62:11-12; Ps 97; Titus 3:4-7

"Let us go, then, to Bethlehem to see this thing that has taken place."

Luke's gospel draws a calming, idyllic scene: a star-filled night with angel song, first-time parents adoring their beautiful baby boy, and local shepherds sharing the joy.

In contrast, the hectic days that lead up to Christmas are jarring for many. Years ago I heard a story about a little girl on Christmas Eve. The Christmas rush was on and the little girl was brimming over with excitement. Her mother was frantically running from task to task. Her father was resentful, being ordered back and forth to various stores for last-minute needs. The little girl seemed to be in everyone's way. Her mother ignored her interruptions, her father had no time for her questions, and her older brother just shooed her away.

By bedtime, the little five-year old was thoroughly disappointed and unnerved. When she knelt down to pray the Lord's Prayer, this is what came out: "Forgive us our Christmases as we forgive those who Christmas against us."

Before this day gets too far gone, make it a point to ask forgiveness for your "Christmases" and forgive those who have "Christmased" against you. You'll have a holier, merrier day.

How can I help to make Christmas a true celebration of joy and goodness for those around me?

December 28

Feast of the Holy Family

Roy Goetz

Lectionary 17A
Luke 2:22-40

Sir 3:2-6, 12-14; Ps 128; Col 3:12-21

The child grew and became strong, filled with wisdom; and the favor of God was upon him.

For much of the world, Christmas is over. One of the complaints we often hear the day or two after Christmas is, "It sure was an awful lot of trouble for just a few minutes of tearing packages open." Some people feel a great letdown the day after Christmas. For us as Catholics, the Christmas season has just begun and doesn't end until we celebrate the Baptism of Our Lord.

The readings for this season call our attention to truths that extend well beyond singular events. We hear that Mary and Joseph present Jesus at the Temple, but the end of today's passage draws us into what will be in the life of the

Holy Family. Within the love of his family, the Christ child grows and becomes strong and wise. He is favored by God.

If we are tempted to be a little down following the singular event of Christmas morning, perhaps we can enter more into the "what will be." Within the love of our families and friends, we too are called to grow and become wise and to seek favor with God.

What can I do to grow in strength and wisdom?

January 4

Epiphany of Our Lord

Gregory C. Wolfe

Lectionary 20ABC
Matt 2:1-12

Isa 60:1-6; Ps 72; Eph 3:2-3a, 5-6

. . . behold, magi from the east arrived in Jerusalem, saying, "Where is the newborn king of the Jews?"

Encouragement sometimes comes from unexpected places. In the Gospel of Matthew, the magi surprise all of Jerusalem when they arrive from the east looking for the newborn king. Exactly who the magi were, we do not know; but it would seem they did not share the Jewish faith. Instead they appear to be followers of astrology, studying the heavens to find understanding and guidance for their lives. How wonderful that they who did not share the faith of the Hebrews would be led by nature to seek and eventually find the Messiah.

In our own time, I am reminded of a number of physicists who have journeyed through atheism to arrive at a belief in God, and in some cases, have even found Christ. They have studied both the tiniest world of the atom and the greatest expanses of the universe. After searching, they found a surprise at the end of their intellectual journey.

To complete the tale of the magi, there is a legend that years later St. Thomas traveled east and found the magi still living. Hearing of the life, death, and resurrection of Jesus, they were overjoyed and were baptized as Christians. Such possibilities I find encouraging.

When has my own searching led me to unexpected treasures that enrich my faith?

Baptism of the Lord

Clifford M. Yeary

Lectionary 21B
Mark 1:7-11

Isa 42:1-4, 6-7; Ps 29; Acts 10:34-38

"I am not worthy to stoop and loosen the thongs of his sandals."

Loosening the thongs of sandals was the job of a servant, most commonly a slave. Keep in mind that this claim of unworthiness comes from John, the guy who shouted out the sins of kings to shame them in public (Matt 14:3-4). John has humility. He does know his place: he has come on the scene to call all Israel to repentance through baptism, from highest nobility to humblest urchin. So why does he baptize Jesus, if John is so unworthy to be in his presence? Why would Jesus submit to a baptism of repentance?

When people came out of the Jordan after being baptized by John, they were part of a new Israel, an Israel that was now offering itself as a pure and obedient servant of God. This was to be the Israel God would once again call, "my son" (see Hos 11:1). Jesus' baptism unites him with God's people in a special way. He is the one to whom God says, "You are my beloved Son." Because he is the Son, when we are baptized in him, we share in his Spirit, and we too are told, "You are my beloved child, in whom I am well pleased."

Am I aware of my special relationship to God as a beloved child?

January 18

Second Sunday in Ordinary Time

Susan McCarthy, RDC

Lectionary 65B *1 Sam 3:3b-10; Ps 40; 1 Cor 6:13c-15a, 17-20*
John 1:35-42

"What are you looking for?"

One way a spiritual director tries to learn how God is acting in our lives is by asking us what we are looking for, what we are seeking. What we are looking for on a retreat or at a particular time in our lives may be an indication of what God is trying to speak to our hearts.

The more we can clearly know and express what we are seeking the better able a director is to help us find our way.

Unfortunately, it is not always clear to us what we are looking for. Most often, I think, we are looking for peace, for joy, and perhaps for authenticity. We are looking for those qualities that lead us closer to God.

The founder of my religious congregation, Mary Caroline Dannat Starr, was not even aware she was looking for something when she was drawn as a young girl into a church in lower Manhattan by the sound of an organ playing. In responding to the call to go into the church, she began a lifelong love affair with God.

So what is it I am looking for in my life?

January 25

Third Sunday in Ordinary Time

Monsignor David LeSieur

Lectionary 68B
Mark 1:14-20

Jonah 3:1-5, 10; Ps 25; 1 Cor 7:29-31

They abandoned their nets and followed him.

Jesus' first demand in Mark's gospel is "Repent, and believe in the gospel." This is a radical demand because repentance implies abandoning one's former ways of living and making decisions.

Jesus next tells Simon, Andrew, James, and John, all fishermen, to be his disciples. "They abandoned their nets and followed him . . . they left their father . . . and followed him." We can admire such willingness on the part of these disciples to leave their familiar ways and cast their lot with an itinerant preacher.

But have they really accepted the good news of the kingdom? Have they changed? Not necessarily. The remainder of Mark's gospel will show just how difficult it is for the followers of Jesus to accept his message and pattern their lives and decisions by that message.

When a couple says "I do" on their wedding day, they mean it, but have little idea of the demands of living that promise "for better or for worse." The same was true for the disciples. They dropped their nets willingly enough, perhaps naively expecting a new adventure, but discovered how hard are the demands of abandoning, not just nets, but one's very self to the expectations of someone else.

What fears are preventing me from leaving behind my "nets" to follow Jesus more completely?

February 1

Fourth Sunday in Ordinary Time

Dan Borlik, CM

Lectionary 71B
Mark 1:21-28

Deut 18:15-20; Ps 95; 1 Cor 7:32-35

"He commands even the unclean spirits and they obey him."

Clearly, Jesus knew his own people well and loved them. Yet, from the very beginning of his public ministry, Jesus seems to have dealt with a tough crowd! Whether in the streets or the synagogue, he willingly faced a mixed and conflicted audience. Some open and others hostile, many were divided as cliques for all kinds of political and religious reasons, and most were likely to be (then as today) personally wounded, conflicted, and searching for salvation.

But for whomever truly listened to Jesus, he was far more than a persuasive and compassionate teacher. His own actions mirrored his words and gave him authority.

Most strikingly, Mark's gospel states that those most wounded and particularly those enslaved by evil could immediately recognize Jesus for who he was. At this moment early on in Jesus' ministry even the possessing demons found the clarity to respond to his commands in obedience. But what of all the others in the crowd?

As one of Christ's people today, am I listening to him? How will I give him authority today . . . over me, over my life?

February 8

Fifth Sunday in Ordinary Time

Cackie Upchurch

Lectionary 74B
Mark 1:29-39

Job 7:1-4, 6-7; Ps 147; 1 Cor 9:16-19, 22-23

"Everyone is looking for you."

I wonder if Jesus ever felt overwhelmed by the attention he was receiving as he ministered. People looked for him hoping to be healed, they looked for him curious to see a wonder-worker, and they looked for him to challenge his authority. No doubt some were jealous of him, but many were in awe.

In this gospel passage Jesus is at home in Capernaum where people recognize him, and yet they seem to be getting to know him truly for the first time. He demonstrates compassion without pity, and a sense of purpose without ambition. He recognizes the need in front of him and he addresses it. For Peter's mother-in-law that meant healing.

Jesus is the "go to" man of the day. And his "day" occurred not just in the ancient villages around Galilee. His day continues even to our own time. Every time we look for him, we are affirming that we want to see with our eyes what he has done for others and will do for us. We are looking for him anticipating that he will recognize our need.

When I look for Jesus, what disposition do I bring? Am I confident, curious, anxious, or doubting? Will I receive what he has to give me?

February 15

Sixth Sunday in Ordinary Time

Robert L. Morris

Lectionary 77B
Mark 1:40-45

Lev 13:1-2, 44-46; Ps 32; 1 Cor 10:31–11:1

"If you wish, you can make me clean."

Many people are crippled; others suffer from life-threatening ailments. The leper that Jesus encountered lived with a disease that deprived him of living a normal life. If there were so many with sickness and disease, why did Jesus not heal all those that he met who were suffering?

During Jesus' ministry, healing the sick and afflicted was a clear sign of God's presence. These acts of compassion were simply announcements that something greater was about to unfold. His passion and death on the cross and his resurrection and ascension into heaven gave new meaning to life and a deeper insight into the meaning of suffering.

Because Jesus gives us the gift of himself, we come to realize that we no longer suffer alone. With his help, we now have the confidence that Jesus is forever present to us, helping us to understand his promise that through suffering we can look forward to a more meaningful existence beyond the one in which we live. With Jesus at our side, suffering is an opportunity to prepare ourselves for new life.

"I do will it. Be made clean."

When has personal suffering helped me to ask Jesus for what I truly need?

February 22

Seventh Sunday in Ordinary Time

Roy Goetz

Lectionary 80B *Isa 43:18-19, 21-22, 24b-25; Ps 41; 2 Cor 1:18-22* Mark 2:1-12

When Jesus saw their faith . . .

I once worked for a high school principal who believed that schools too often set their sights on mediocrity and hit it dead center every time. I am a teacher, and I know this can be true—sometimes we expect too little of our students. We may also, at times, expect too little in our relationships with our husband or wife, with our children, with family and friends as well. This attitude can creep into our spiritual life.

Do we really believe Christianity can transform the world we live in, or are our expectations not that high? Perhaps complacency in our faith flows from low expectations easily fulfilled.

The paralytic in today's gospel surely had some expectations as his friends brought him to see Jesus. Jesus saw their faith and far exceeded their expectations. The paralyzed man received much more than he could have imagined. He was healed physically, but much more important than that, he was cleansed of his sins. When we come to Jesus, what do we expect? No matter what we desire, Jesus will exceed our expectations. We should be astounded that such a love has come to us.

Do I put limits on what I expect from Jesus?

February 25

Ash Wednesday

Lilly Hess

Lectionary 219 *Joel 2:12-18; Ps 51; 2 Cor 5:20–6:2*
Matt 6:1-6, 16-18

"Jesus said to his disciples . . ."

In these verses of Matthew's gospel, Jesus is asking us to pay attention to how we give alms, pray, and fast. It is so easy to pray without hearing what we're saying, to expect more of others, and to fast without losing or gaining anything. Lent is a good time to look at these practices in new ways and see how they might enrich our relationship with God and others.

Begin with prayer. Pray for your community as you gather for Sunday liturgy. Look at people you are gathered with and say a little prayer for each, like "God be with you this day." Really listen to what you are saying as you sing and pray aloud with the congregation.

Fasting is doing without something, usually food. Consider giving up complaining, and take delight in eating your food. Savor its richness and thank God for those who brought it to your table.

Give money or time to groups who feed the hungry in your community. Another way of giving alms might be to give words of encouragement and thanks to those you meet as you move through your day—family members, coworkers, clerks in stores.

Enter Lent with a joyful heart and a plan of action!

What plan of action will I make as I enter into this holy season? Will my plan lead to more joy in my life?

First Sunday of Lent

Rosa María Icaza, CCVI

Lectionary 23B
Mark 1:12-15

Gen 9:8-15; Ps 25; 1 Pet 3:18-22

He was among wild beasts, and the angels ministered to him.

It is interesting to hear that the Spirit drove Jesus into the desert and yet Jesus was tempted by Satan there. Sometimes we are advised to go to a deserted place to flee from worldly attractions and to be more deeply present to God's inspirations (see Hos 2:16). We usually complain of being distracted at prayer time and use this fact as an excuse to abandon prayer. Jesus gives us a different example. "He remained in the desert for forty days"!

In spite of difficult temptations symbolized by "wild beasts," Jesus persevered in prayer and fasting. His strength was found in his Father's love; God sent angels to minister to him. Even in the midst of great difficulties and sufferings, we know God is always with us and his angels are those persons and circumstances that console, encourage, and strengthen our spirit.

Jesus urges us to change our ways and follow his teachings, particularly during the holy season of Lent, so we can be ready when he comes to encounter us in a special way at

Easter. We renew our baptismal promises not only in words but also in the way we lead our Christian life.

When have I experienced God's ministering angels in the midst of trials?

March 8

Second Sunday of Lent

Jerre Roberts

Lectionary 26B *Gen 22:1-2, 9a, 10-13, 15-18; Ps 116; Rom 8:31b-34* Mark 9:2-10

Suddenly, looking around, they no longer saw anyone but Jesus alone with them.

The account of the Transfiguration is recorded by each of the three synoptic gospel writers—Matthew, Mark, and Luke. We hear this story every year on the Second Sunday of Lent. This should alert us to the importance of this event in the lives of the apostles and in our lives today.

The three disciples looked around and saw Jesus in the fullness of his glory. They realized that they were in their deepest being ALONE with him, regardless of outward circumstances. This is the essence of Christian faith. Christ is Lord; he is the totality of faith.

Prayer and meditation foster this clarity of vision. It might require going apart from the everyday, "up to a high mountain," whether that high mountain is a prolonged time of retreat or simply the faithful practice of daily devotion.

Every year a friend of mine makes her New Year's resolutions on the feast of the Epiphany because, she says, too many resolutions are broken in the first week of the year. Perhaps this works for her. The Second Sunday of Lent is not too late for us to begin anew and resolve to make time to spend alone with Jesus on a daily basis.

How is my prayer life giving me the opportunity to experience the fullness of glory in Jesus?

March 15

Third Sunday of Lent

Jerome Kodell, OSB

Lectionary 29B
John 2:13-25

Exod 20:1-17; Ps 19; 1 Cor 1:22-25

Since the Passover of the Jews was near, Jesus went up to Jerusalem.

This is the first of three celebrations of the Passover mentioned in the Gospel of John (see also 6:4; 13:1). John goes out of his way to connect the Passover with the mission of

Jesus. Jesus is introduced very early as the (paschal) Lamb of God (1:29), and the culmination of his mission is connected with the third Passover: "Before the feast of Passover, Jesus knew that his hour had come to pass from this world to the Father" (13:1).

John's chronology of Holy Week differs from that of the other gospel writers: for them, the Last Supper is the Passover meal of that year, but in John's narrative the supper takes place a day before the beginning of Passover, so that Jesus is hanging on the cross while the lambs are being slaughtered for the Passover meal. Jesus does not eat the Passover lamb, but is the Passover lamb.

The cleansing of the Temple in John's version symbolizes that Jesus himself has replaced the Jerusalem Temple. By drawing attention to this first Passover and the replacement theme, the evangelist is pointing us forward to another Passover when Jesus will "go up to Jerusalem" to replace the traditional lamb.

How does the feast of Passover help me to appreciate the role of Jesus in our salvation?

March 22

Fourth Sunday of Lent

Mary J. Glynn, SJC

Lectionary 32B *2 Chr 36:14-16, 19-23; Ps 137; Eph 2:4-10*
John 3:14-21

"But whoever lives the truth comes to the light."

The journey of faith for catechumens and candidates contains many opportunities to make choices. Nicodemus reminds us that conversion is gradual and that God's love is always there to sustain us. God invites us to enter into a personal relationship with him but continues the invitation to deepen that relationship in discipleship.

Nicodemus listened to Jesus, saw his actions, and believed that Jesus came from God. Then he chose to seek out Jesus under the cover of darkness and enter into dialogue with him. He was willing to speak to Jesus and to be engaged by him and then to actively seek ways to follow him.

Discipleship is not static; it is ongoing and dynamic. Discipleship is a daily response to the invitation to deepen our relationship with Jesus and the Christian community. It is not a one-time assent to a set of dogmatic formulas, but a lifelong attitude of openness to journey from darkness to light each day as we choose to share more deeply in Christ's life, passion, and death. It is pure gift as we trust that God's love journeys with us to the light as we open ourselves to be true disciples.

Do I seek to live the truth of the Good News? Where does my life give evidence of this?

March 29

Fifth Sunday of Lent

Frank Zanoff

Lectionary 35B
John 12:20-33

Jer 31:31-34; Ps 51; Heb 5:7-9

Some Greeks who had come to worship at the Passover Feast came to Philip . . . and asked him, "Sir, we would like to see Jesus."

The Greeks were hoping for an encounter with Jesus and sought out Philip, a man with a Greek name, as an intermediary. As we look back on the gospel narrative we hear how they were blessed to hear Jesus foretell that he would be lifted up, and like a grain of wheat, have to die to bear much fruit.

As this Lenten season draws to a close we would be well served to take an inventory and discern how we've taken advantage of and how appreciative we are of our opportunities to have an encounter with Christ. Do we see the presence of Christ in the liturgy we celebrate and in the priest presider? Do we feel the presence of Christ in Sacred Scripture as it is proclaimed? Do we encounter Christ in the person next to us at Mass, in the checkout line, or in the car that cuts us off in traffic?

If this Lent has been a growing experience for us in all these areas, then we are as close to Christ as the Greeks were two thousand years ago.

During this Lenten season, how have I encountered Christ?

April 5

Palm Sunday

Macrina Wiederkehr, OSB

Lectionary 38B *Isa 50:4-7; Ps 22; Phil 2:6-11*
Mark 11:1-10 (Lectionary 37B, Procession with Palms)

Those preceding him as well as those following kept crying out: "Hosanna!"

As I envisioned the original Palm Sunday procession, Jesus on a donkey seems strange. Had I been directing this liturgical procession I would have chosen a white stallion. Yet the donkey fits the humble stance of this Servant Leader, so different from the great ones of this earth.

We broke off branches from palm trees, waving them with loving excitement proclaiming him our King. A spirit of praise pervaded the atmosphere. Love ran wild. Well! We thought it was love!

Looking back on all of this now that the mood changed for the Good Friday procession I wonder, what happened? How could those who were waving palm branches with such devotion slink into the crowd as silent spectators on Good Friday? How could their joy become indifference, fear, betrayal, and even hate?

As a twenty-first-century person reflecting on this I, too, find myself wondering about the processions in my life that begin with joyful presence, yet end with unconscious living. In my daily communion procession to receive the Bread of Life I often experience a contemplative stirring. Yet as my procession through the day begins my fervor falls away.

Has something happened to that first movement of the Spirit in my life? What happened between my Palm Sunday and Good Friday?

April 9

Mass of the Lord's Supper

Judy Hoelzeman

Lectionary 39ABC *Exod 12:1-8, 11-14; Ps 116; 1 Cor 11:23-26*
John 13:1-15

Peter said to him, "You will never wash my feet."

What's new? The Eucharist.

Savor the familiar in today's gospel, but be ready to be surprised by God's Word as well. This reading is considered to parallel the other three evangelists' accounts of the institution of the Eucharist. However, John stresses, not the formula and ritual, but the Eucharist as a journey of service and conversion.

The Last Supper began Jesus' journey into his passion, death, and resurrection. In giving himself at the Passover meal, Jesus offered the apostles an escape from their spiritually dead past. That meal set the apostles (and us) on a journey of conversion and new life. The Eucharist, then, is always changing, as we leave our dead past and strike out into the unknown, always trying to move closer and closer to Jesus.

Peter was the first to challenge and try to control Jesus' gift. In the end he had the humility to say "yes" to the surprising and painful truth that Jesus was going to save the world through service, even unto death.

God's miracle of the Eucharist at the Passover meal was brief. Jesus' command to imitate him in washing others' feet is for a lifetime.

How can the celebration of these holy days help me to surrender to God's call to service?

April 10

Good Friday

Monsignor J. Gaston Hebert

Lectionary 40ABC *Isa 52:13–53:12; Ps 31; Heb 4:14-16; 5:7-9*
John 18:1–19:42

Then [Pilate] handed him over to them to be crucified.

The enormity of God's love is humbling and staggering. It's difficult to grasp all that Jesus was willing to suffer for our salvation. The crucifix reminds Catholics: "No one has greater love than this, to lay down one's life for one's friends" (John 15:13). His was the absolute, total gift, the surrender of his life, the shedding of his blood, out of sheer unmitigated, personal love. The recognition of this gift should evoke a deep love for Jesus.

How could anyone have the effrontery to insult the source of all love? The triple denial of Peter and the sellout by Judas, and the insults and taunts of the crowd that Jesus endured from the time of his arrest to the moment of his death, evoke embarrassed sadness that people could respond so ungratefully to the love of Jesus.

Our embarrassment stems from the recognition that our sins set the stage for the death of Jesus. Jesus died for OUR salvation. When we wish to cushion our words, we might say: "Now, don't take this personally, but . . . ." On the contrary, in order to understand the love of God, we must take the crucifixion very personally.

How does meditating on the crucifix help me to grow spiritually? How does the crucifix direct my gaze when I look for meaning in daily living?

April 11

Easter Vigil

Clifford M. Yeary

Lectionary 41B
Mark 16:1-7

Exod 14:15–15:1; Ps 30; Rom 6:3-11 (and other readings)

"Do not be amazed!"

Yeah, right! I suppose the angel's words lost something in translation. I don't know how well angel translates into English, let alone Aramaic or Greek. Personally, I think this would be a good paraphrase for what the angel meant: "Be full of wonder, let awe play up and down your spine like a timpani. Just do not fail to believe." Jesus is risen, he is risen indeed!

This is the pinnacle moment, the climax of the gospel. The women, immersed in their sorrow, do not succumb to denial. They embrace their grief wholly; they will mourn through a true act of love and devotion by anointing his body. Worried that even this doleful act will be frustrated by the stone that separates the living from the dead, they find that the tomb is not only open, it has become conjoined with heaven. An angel announces what cannot be believed but which must.

I have grieved in this life. I will assume that you have, too. The angel's announcement is the answer to all sorrow. Don't look for him here, but do go out and tell others to look for him. They will find him, just as he promised, and so will we.

Who can I tell to look for the one who has risen from the dead?

April 12

Easter Sunday

Cackie Upchurch

Lectionary 42ABC
John 20:1-9

Acts 10:34a, 37-43; Ps 118; Col 3:1-4

He saw and believed.

What did the disciple believe when he saw burial cloths rolled up and put aside, and there was no body to be found? It would be logical to think something dastardly had occurred. Could his body have been stolen? Was this one last sign of disrespect for the man from Galilee who offered his life?

Only those who had wandered the roads with Jesus as he ministered could possibly have suspected that the appearance of grave robbery could mean something altogether different. Perhaps as word spread, even those who had been touched by his words or his actions would begin to open their imaginations to the unthinkable—he was no longer in the grave because he was risen from the dead.

The followers of Jesus brought physical sight to the tomb, but more importantly, they brought insight with them that was the result of being shaped in the presence of Jesus. Faith can indeed be rooted in physical realities—there was an empty tomb—but it must make the leap where our physical senses can only point with wonder. This leap is one that trusts in God's surprises.

In this Easter season, where is God asking me to leap in trust toward a new awareness?

Second Sunday of Easter or Divine Mercy Sunday

Gregory C. Wolfe

Lectionary 44B
John 20:19-31

Acts 4:32-35; Ps 118; 1 John 5:1-6

The disciples rejoiced when they saw the Lord.

Saint Raymond of Peñafort, Spain, was a wonderful Dominican priest and canon lawyer in the thirteenth century. He wrote that suffering can come to the followers of Christ like blows from a two-edged sword. One edge made from outside conflicts, the other from interior fears.

Hiding in Jerusalem, the disciples of Jesus are under attack from the two-edged sword. Fearing those who had been involved in the death of their leader, they had locked the doors. Arrest, imprisonment, and even death were real possibilities for them outside those doors. How could the disciples possibly get out of this place?

Inside, the disciples were gripped with fear. Understandably terrified, I imagine they were also confused, angry, resentful, depressed. What were they supposed to do now?

For the times when the two-edged sword is raining down on Christians, St. Raymond provides this advice: look then on Jesus. See for yourselves that Jesus was sinless, yet suffered, and give thanks to God for blessings received.

Is this not how the disciples were saved from their exterior threat and internal fears? For Jesus came and stood in their midst and said, "Peace be with you." And the disciples rejoiced when they saw the Lord.

When I have felt fearful or angry, how has it helped me to focus on Jesus?

April 26

Third Sunday of Easter

Susan McCarthy, RDC

Lectionary 47B
Luke 24:35-48

Acts 3:13-15, 17-19; Ps 4; 1 John 2:1-5a

Then he opened their minds to understand the Scriptures.

The Merriam-Webster's Dictionary provides three meanings for the verb *to understand*. It is to grasp the meaning of, to have a thorough or technical acquaintance with or expertness in the practice, or to be thoroughly familiar with the character. These definitions fit well with the invitation offered to us in this single verse of today's gospel. Through our reading and profound reflection on the Scriptures we are able to truly come to know who Jesus is and what his expectations are for those of us who follow him as disciples.

The famous quote of St. Jerome in the fourth century, "Ignorance of Scripture is ignorance of Christ," speaks clearly to the importance of reading, knowing, and understanding God's Word to us each day in order that we may become true disciples.

How fortunate we have been in the last forty-five years since Vatican II to have the Scriptures made more and more available to us through clear translations, good scholarship in commentaries, and study editions of the Bible.

We now see that God does speak to us in real and personal ways. The Word welcomes, comforts, challenges, and invites us to respond.

How am I taking advantage of access to the Scriptures? In what ways do I try to deepen my understanding?

May 3

Fourth Sunday of Easter

Nancy Lee Walters

Lectionary 50B
John 10:11-18

Acts 4:8-12; Ps 118; 1 John 3:1-2

"I am the good shepherd."

In this reading we're told in detail the qualities required of a good shepherd: care, devotion, commitment, and concern.

Then there are the not so good qualities of one who merely tends sheep: being neglectful and irresponsible.

We have family friends that tend a small flock of sheep. While visiting the family and talking with the primary flock tender I laughingly referred to her as a shepherdess. In truth, Crystal is a good shepherd. The sheep are surrounded by an electric fence to protect them from predators and prevent them from wandering into harm's way. They are fed healthy food and given fresh water so they will thrive. If one of the flock shows signs of illness or injury a veterinarian is called or Crystal tends to the problem. There is always someone around the farm to tend the flock. Perhaps Crystal's attention to her flock is no more than anyone should expect of a shepherd, but I think the qualities she shows in her day-to-day work are much like Jesus the Good Shepherd.

We can lead our daily life by being devoted to our family, committed to our work, and showing concern to all we encounter just as a good shepherd would.

When have I felt God's direction and protection? Has God's shepherding care for me helped me to care for others more deeply?

Fifth Sunday of Easter

Roy Goetz

Lectionary 53B
John 15:1-8

Acts 9:26-31; Ps 22; 1 John 3:18-24

"Whoever remains in me and I in him will bear much fruit."

We have all probably had the experience of driving a familiar road and arriving at our destination but not remembering the trip—or reading to the bottom of a page and not having any idea what we just read. Sometimes we do things without really thinking. When reading, this is probably OK most of the time; when driving, not great, but in our relationships with others, no good at all.

Often we hear that communication is the most important part of a marriage. If we are not really listening, we can be sure our spouse will let us know. If we want a relationship to grow, we have to give ourselves over to it completely—we have to connect with the other person.

We can be sure this holds true in our relationship with Jesus. We must know that we can do nothing unless Jesus lives in us, and we live in him. If we are not connected to the true vine, we cannot bear good fruit. We must make a conscious effort to ask Jesus to be a part of everything we say and do, so that we might truly be his disciples and bring glory to God.

How strongly am I attached to the true vine?

May 17

Sixth Sunday of Easter

Dan Hennessey

Lectionary 56B *Acts 10:25-26, 34-35, 44-48; Ps 98; 1 John 4:7-10*
John 15:9-17

"This I command you: love one another."

All of God's revelation boils down to three little words found in 1 John 4:8, "God is love." As Christians, what should be our response to that simple summary of the faith? Jesus answers that question for us in today's gospel in equally simple words, "Love one another as I love you." While his words are few, their implications for us are enormous.

This type of love calls us to action and not necessarily with the warm, fuzzy sentiments commonly associated with romantic and familial love. It is a love that is self-sacrificing service to others. We might consider this too difficult, assuming we're no modern-day saint. But we can find examples of this kind of love in the ordinary human existence we all share. The parents who work an extra shift so their teen can go to the prom. The homemaker who volunteers at the shelter. The coworker who shares lunch when ours was forgotten. The retiree who spurns the golf course for a visit with an elderly neighbor.

This is how we lay down our life for others, by making routine daily sacrifices. In doing so, we bring the love that is God to all those around us.

When have I experienced the benefit of someone else's service on my behalf? Did I recognize God in that experience?

May 24

Seventh Sunday of Easter

Jerre Roberts

Lectionary 60B *Acts 1:15-17, 20a, 20c-26; Ps 103; 1 John 4:11-16*
John 17:11b-19

"Consecrate them in truth. Your word is truth."

Jesus' prayer for his disciples at the Last Supper is also his eternal prayer for us. When we think of prayer, we imagine it is something that we do. Undeniably our prayer life is essential in keeping us connected to God. We pray to talk to God, to offer our petitions; we meditate to listen to God, to hear his voice. But are we really aware that Jesus is also praying *for* us to his Father? It is an awesome thought!

What does Jesus pray for us? That we know the truth, that we be consecrated in the truth. The dictionary defines truth as that which corresponds to fact or reality. Indeed, truth, and reality, has been defined by the world and for the world as a scientifically provable entity. We as Christians realize that this definition is inadequate. There is a deeper truth, a truth that is not so obvious in the "world's" eyes, a truth that flows directly from God. The eyes of faith apprehend a deeper reality.

As we seek this truth, we can be consoled and strengthened by the thought that it is not entirely up to us—Jesus supports us by his prayers.

In my search for truth, am I open to God's gift of insight? Do I trust in God's desire to guide me in truth?

May 21 or May 24

The Ascension of the Lord

Clifford M. Yeary

Lectionary 58B
Mark 16:15-20

Acts 1:1-11; Ps 47; Eph 1:17-23

They will speak new languages . . .

I believe in the Gospel, but I'm not very big on handling snakes—or drinking poison, for that matter. There is a new language I am learning to speak, however. It's not quite "speaking in tongues," but it is a language of faith.

Jesus' ascension is so much more than the visual oddity of seeing his feet disappear through a cloud. However quaintly it may have been depicted in the past, this all-important event between Easter and Pentecost is worth pondering in our hearts. Jesus has taken our humanity and nestled it forever in the bosom of God. And now that humanity has a permanent home in God, God's Spirit is free to flow into human hearts here on earth.

Even as my body ages and weariness comes earlier every day, there is an unbounded joy to be had in just being human! Grasping ahold of this in faith and attempting to talk or write about it forces me to realize that my gifts of language have been shattered, and yet the truth is there, so I must learn a new language to proclaim it to all in the world, especially my loved ones.

What sign or wonder accompanies my faith?

May 31

Pentecost

Macrina Wiederkehr, OSB

Lectionary 63B
John 20:19-23

Acts 2:1-11; Ps 104; 1 Cor 12:3b-7, 12-13

Jesus came and stood in their midst and said to them, "Peace be with you."

The Pentecost story, flowing out of biblical history and told in various ways, is a treasured page in Christian faith. In our gospel for today we see the friends of Jesus fearfully huddled behind locked doors. When Jesus breaks through those locked doors with greetings of peace, something happens to their apprehensive hearts. As their courage and joy blossom we can well imagine how those hearts catch fire and grow wings of hope and peace. Jesus breathes on them and sends them forth, allowing the space between the words of this story to have a voice. I can almost hear the transforming breath of Jesus.

That breath is still sending us forth. We, too, know the anxiety of waiting behind walls of fear. We need daily reminders that help is just a breath away. There is always something in our hearts ready to explode with love, ready to catch fire, ready to be at peace; but we have to be very quiet to feel the movement. Then after the Spirit breathes into us and flames out of us, we must learn to go back to the *quiet center within* and wait again. It's the only way to keep the Spirit alive and breathing in us.

How does my daily adventure with the Spirit of Jesus keep the Pentecost story alive?

June 7

Solemnity of the Most Holy Trinity

John Hall

Lectionary 165B
Matt 28:16-20

Deut 4:32-34, 39-40; Ps 33; Rom 8:14-17

When they all saw him, they worshiped.

The phrase "carrots and sticks" is sometimes used to describe positive and negative sources of motivation. In today's gospel, Jesus uses a carrot with his disciples.

This reading is found at the end of Matthew's gospel. Jesus had been crucified, entombed, and only Mary Magdalene and the other Mary find the empty tomb. Jesus appears to the women and directs them to send the apostles to Galilee where he'll meet them. The disciples of Jesus were scared, they had gone into hiding, and didn't know what to do. Everything Jesus told them was now in question. The disciples needed a carrot. Jesus appears to them, reminds them of the task to which they have been called, and he reassures them he will be with them always.

As we celebrated the Christmas holidays this past year, Jesus offered me a carrot. Our college-aged children returned home and all chairs at the supper table were again occupied. Laughter and stories complemented our meals. Love, respect, and admiration among the children were evident. What a blessing that was for my wife and me! We, like the apostles, have been offered a glimpse of the kingdom of God and our faith is affirmed.

Am I prepared this week for God to offer me a sign of the kingdom, a sign to encourage my faith?

June 14

The Solemnity of the Most Holy Body and Blood of Christ

Gregory C. Wolfe

Lectionary 168B
Mark 14:12-16, 22-26

Exod 24:3-8; Ps 116; Heb 9:11-15

This is my blood of the covenant, which will be shed for many.

At the Last Supper, Jesus shows us that the love of God cannot be limited, even by time. For in Jesus, the past, present, and future all come together.

During the course of the Passover meal with his disciples, Jesus gives them the traditional unleavened bread but declares the seemingly impossible: "This is my body." When giving the cup he claims, "This is my blood of the covenant," adding, "which will be shed for many." How could this be? At that moment, the death and resurrection of the Lord had not yet occurred! Nevertheless, Jesus was able to make present at the Last Supper what was still to come: the sacrificed body and blood of the Lamb of God.

During his last Passover supper, Jesus reached back through time and connected with the entire history of the Hebrew people and their covenant relationship with God. Jesus was also present with the disciples in their particular hour and shared with them at table. But most wondrous of all, Jesus reached forward in time to his passion, death, and resurrection in order to offer the very gift of himself to those who would believe in him in every time and place.

In what ways do I experience Jesus as Lord of the past, present, and future?

June 21

Twelfth Sunday in Ordinary Time

Nancy Lee Walters

Lectionary 95B
Mark 4:35-41

Job 38:1, 8-11; Ps 107; 2 Cor 5:14-17

"Why are you terrified?"

These words from Mark's gospel were racing through my head ten years ago on the occasion of my first trip floating Arkansas' Spring River in a canoe with my husband. I'm not afraid of water, but I was very apprehensive of water that was rushing down over rocks with no way to control the canoe to safety. "Don't you care that we might drown?" My husband replied something like "Be still . . . I'm doing the best I can."

Obviously we didn't drown. We did get bruises from sliding down the rocks, but once the canoe was turned right side up, the rest of the trip was very smooth and not a bit terrifying. In retrospect, it was a great trip and one we probably would try again now that we have a little experience.

I imagine the little boat that carried Jesus and the disciples was equipped with some safety measures. Weren't some of the disciples fishermen who had knowledge about sailing in stormy seas? Their great concern was the sudden violence of the storm and that Jesus, their teacher, wasn't as upset. Jesus wanted them to have faith that they and their boat were safe.

What terrifying experiences have given me the opportunity to test my reliance on Jesus' presence and his care?

June 28

Thirteenth Sunday in Ordinary Time

Monsignor David LeSieur

Lectionary 98B *Wis 1:13-15; 2:23-24; Ps 30; 2 Cor 8:7, 9, 13-15*
Mark 5:21-43

"Do not be afraid; just have faith."

This episode begins with Jesus crossing the Sea of Galilee "to the other side." It is here that Jairus meets him with the news of his daughter's sickness and his request that Jesus heal her.

"Crossing to the other side" can imply passage over frightening depths or fearful distances: from sin to repentance, from faithlessness to trust, from sickness to health, from death to life. Jairus asks Jesus to see his daughter safely to the other side of her sickness. But then comes the report that she has died: "Why trouble the teacher any longer?" Discouragement and fear—not doubt—are the opposites of biblical faith and can stop our progress from where we are to where we need to be.

"Do not be afraid; just have faith," says Jesus, reminding Jairus that the other side is not far away, that the girl is only asleep. The mourners laugh at the idea, but Jesus takes her hand and leads her to safety.

Later Jesus himself will cross to the other side of death, accompanied only by his trust in his Father's will.

When have I experienced a crossing from discouragement to faith? Can I continue to trust that Jesus will make the crossing with me?

July 5

Fourteenth Sunday in Ordinary Time

Cackie Upchurch

Lectionary 101B
Mark 6:1-6

Ezek 2:2-5; Ps 123; 2 Cor 12:7-10

He was amazed at their lack of faith.

In the Gospel of Mark, lack of faith is a recurring theme. The disciples who are closest to Jesus repeatedly seem too dense to "get" what he is doing. And now, in his "native place" Jesus is unable to perform mighty deeds.

Lack of faith, however, is not an obstacle to Jesus in an ultimate way. He persists with his followers; he continues to offer himself to those who come to see and hear him; and he stands firm when people are offended by him. Ultimately, Jesus shows himself as the Son of God even to those who want him to remain a simple carpenter born of Mary and Joseph, a boy down the street who surely cannot be as wise as he seems.

Perhaps we also amaze Jesus with our lack of faith, or with a lack of trust. But be assured that he will not give up on us or fail to return time and again. Lack of faith on our part does not lead to lack of compassion or forgiveness or healing on Jesus' part. We want Jesus to find in us a home, a native place, but we have to be open to stretching our faith and trusting in him.

What prevents me from seeing Jesus as one who is deserving of my trust? Am I fearful of who he can become and what he might ask of me as I trust him more and more?

July 12

Fifteenth Sunday in Ordinary Time

Dan Borlik, CM

Lectionary 104B
Mark 6:7-13

Amos 7:12-15; Ps 85; Eph 1:3-14

Take nothing for the journey but a walking stick . . .

Jesus in this gospel seems *so radical* with his Twelve! What's the point? That they should always be able to travel light as did the prophets? That "chosen ones" be careful to practice poverty and avoid many possessions? That his disciples (then and now) should avoid putting down roots too deeply during our own short lives? Perhaps.

But Jesus had more in mind than some kind of evangelical caution. After all, he knew that the Twelve would make many, many mistakes. At the base of his teaching and life Jesus offers that lasting happiness and peace which we are missing and which we yearn for. His one passion is to share his Father's love with everyone! Nothing, including the practical details of how to do so, must distract his representatives from sharing the Good News.

What makes sharing the Good News too "complicated" for me? What one piece of protective clothing or useful baggage might I drop by the wayside today?

July 19

Sixteenth Sunday in Ordinary Time

Marie Morris

Lectionary 107B
Mark 6:30-34

Jer 23:1-6; Ps 23; Eph 2:13-18

"Come away by yourselves to a deserted place and rest a while."

My spouse and I recently disproved the old adage "you learn from your mistakes" when, on an extended autumn getaway, we repeated a mistake we have made before by overloading our days with multiple activities. Upon returning home, it took several days to recover before we were able to resume our regular routine. Later, reflecting on our trip, we agreed that our favorite moments were those spent camping at the lakeshore, relaxing and listening to the waves, and admiring the autumn colors and beautiful sunsets.

The New Testament relates the times Jesus sought solitude. Jesus understood the need for his disciples to retreat, to be alone in order to be renewed in body and in spirit—"come away . . . to a deserted place and rest a while."

We are all guilty, at one time or another, of being overwhelmed by the busyness we ourselves inject into our everyday lives. We, too, have to withdraw to a quiet place so we can better appreciate God's creation and become more effective ministers of God's Word.

Do I recognize when I need to be renewed spiritually?

July 26

Seventeenth Sunday in Ordinary Time

Judy Hoelzeman

Lectionary 110B
John 6:1-15

2 Kgs 4:42-44; Ps 145; Eph 4:1-6

"There is a boy here who has five barley loaves and two fish; but what good are these for so many?"

We can learn a big lesson from the little boy in today's gospel. Jesus and his disciples had a problem—a tired, hungry crowd—and nothing to feed them. Then the child stepped up and offered his own lunch. We know he was poor because in Jesus' day, only poor people made bread out of barley. As far as we can tell, the boy was there alone, with only enough food for himself. Had his parents been with him, they might have been too timid to offer such a meager gift. But, childlike, their son was proud of what he *could* offer, instead of embarrassed by what he *couldn't*.

Jesus took what the boy gave and worked wonders with it. In the end, everyone in the crowd got more than they needed. Without the child's contribution, the miracle would not have happened.

Just as he needed the boy, God needs us to bring about the miracle of his kingdom on earth. What else does God have to use but our seemingly insignificant efforts? No need to be embarrassed if our offering is small. Be assured it can help Jesus perform a miracle—perhaps even today.

Finding myself in the presence of Jesus, what do I offer him this day to use for building the kingdom of God?

August 2

Eighteenth Sunday in Ordinary Time

Gregory C. Wolfe

Lectionary 113B
John 6:24-35

Exod 16:2-4, 12-15; Ps 78; Eph 4:17, 20-24

"Whoever comes to me will never hunger."

Sometimes what we eat really seems to matter. We don't want a certain food because we had the same thing yesterday or maybe we don't like the taste. At other times, we crave a particular food. We feel nothing else can satisfy us.

What I love are those times when I get to share a meal with someone, and it doesn't matter what we eat. Like dinner with my wife on our wedding anniversary when the two of us can simply be together. Or when an old friend comes to town and the meal gives us a chance to talk. In these cases, the food is not nearly as important as the person.

Jesus showed he understood our physical need to eat. He fed the five thousand. The Lord's Prayer includes a petition for our Father to give us our daily bread. But Jesus also challenges us to work for food that endures. He wants to be certain we also receive from his Father the true bread from heaven which gives life to the world. Ultimately, Jesus wants us to believe in him and come to him through the Eucharist—where the food and the person are one.

How have my hungers been satisfied when I turn to Jesus? Could my prayer time be symbolized by a meal with a dear friend?

August 9

Nineteenth Sunday in Ordinary Time

Lilly Hess

Lectionary 116B
John 6:41-51

1 Kgs 19:4-8; Ps 34; Eph 4:30–5:2

"I am the bread of life."

There is a lot of complaining in these verses about where Jesus came from and where he got his authority. Why were the religious leaders so opposed to Jesus? They questioned his origins and his mission. Inwardly they must have wondered if what Jesus was saying about God was true, but they closed their minds to that truth and refused to believe that Jesus came down from heaven. They just didn't "get it."

Why did some people "get it"? Because they opened their minds to what Jesus was saying and what they experienced of him. He spoke of God's love and mercy. He gave sight to the blind, healed the sick and lame. He walked among them, ate and celebrated with them, prayed with them. He was one with them. So when Jesus said, "I am the bread of life" they could say, "Yes, I have experienced you as bread. You have given me hope and a promise of eternal life."

We too can experience Jesus as the bread of life for ourselves and for our world. We can open ourselves to the good news of Jesus in his words and deeds. In our prayer we can learn to trust in God's love and forgiveness.

Am I among those who "get it" when Jesus continues to speak in the world today? Do I allow my heart to be open and my mind to be transformed?

August 16

Twentieth Sunday in Ordinary Time

Clifford M. Yeary

Lectionary 119B
John 6:51-58

Prov 9:1-6; Ps 34; Eph 5:15-20

"How can this man give us his flesh to eat?"

I think the aroma of hot, home-baked bread fresh from the oven is likely the most wonderful thing I have ever smelled. As intoxicating—as alluring—as bread can be, there is much in today's gospel that warns me the message is not how "yummy" Jesus is.

Jesus isn't campaigning here. He actually scares many of his followers away (see John 6:60). Few scholars doubt the strong link to the Eucharist in Jesus' words, but many also urge us to hear more than the truth concerning the real presence. Jesus is insisting on his humanity; we who believe he is God come to us are not to discount his humanity in any way. His flesh is real, his blood flows red, and we who believe in Jesus must accept him in the fullness of that reality.

There is always a danger that a human Jesus will be discovered to have a human personality, will be utterly Jewish in culture and ethnicity, and actually belong to a specific time and place in history. Could the God of the cosmos come to us in such a limited fashion? Those who feed on him know they have found life.

What makes me hunger for a human Jesus?

August 23

Twenty-first Sunday in Ordinary Time

Robert L. Morris

Lectionary 122B
John 6:60-69

Jos 24:1-2a, 15-17, 18b; Ps 34; Eph 5:21-32

"You have the words of eternal life."

Tom Brokaw, one of America's distinguished journalists, published a book in 2007 entitled *Boom! Voices of the Sixties: Personal Reflections on the '60s & Today.* The book highlights significant events that disrupted, challenged, and in some cases uprooted society's traditional values. The canons of change reverberated throughout the world. Boom!

In his lifetime, Jesus was one of the seemingly unimportant people who significantly impacted society and all cultures. Jesus challenged traditional beliefs. Accepting his words of eternal life was difficult for some, impossible for others.

When Jesus informed his disciples concerning his passion, they became indignant. Accepting the cross as a way of life was difficult at first for his followers to understand. After the risen Lord was taken to be with the Father, they understood.

Many today have difficulty accepting their cross. When the Lord asks, "Will you also go away?" he is lovingly asking us to discover that he is the one who has "the words of eternal life." What he shares with us, the gift of himself, will help us on our journey in life to reach our goal—eternal life. *Boom!*

How have the words of Jesus disrupted my routine and challenged me?

August 30

Twenty-second Sunday in Ordinary Time

Macrina Wiederkehr, OSB

Lectionary 125B *Deut 4:1-2, 6-8; Ps 15; Jas 1:17-18, 21b-22, 27*
Mark 7:1-8, 14-15, 21-23

They observed that some of his disciples ate their meals with unclean, that is, unwashed, hands.

In no way do the words of Jesus in today's gospel make less valid the good advice you were probably given from early childhood: wash your hands before you eat. Of course it is helpful to remember that there are people in our world who have to carry water for miles for the simple necessities of life. The water they bring into their households may need to be used for more important matters than washing hands.

Jesus is attempting to teach us the art of discerning what is essential in life. He wants us to reflect on priorities. And so he dares to call the hecklers—those on the sidelines who make it part of their profession to watch for other people's faults—hypocrites. How easy it is to honor God with our lips because it is the acceptable thing to do in our society, yet to have hearts that are constantly making judgments about others. How easy it is to *"keep the law"* and forget to love.

Guard well your heart the ancestors tell us. The same heart that pours out envy and greed, hatred and evil thoughts has the potential to send forth love and blessings.

When I evaluate my interior life, am I moved to repentance? To change? To deeper reflection?

September 6

Twenty-third Sunday in Ordinary Time

Susan McCarthy, RDC

Lectionary 128B
Mark 7:31-37

Isa 35:4-7a; Ps 146; Jas 2:1-5

***"Ephphatha!"*—that is, "Be opened!"**

The English translation of this Aramaic word is used in the Rite of Baptism (for children) and as part of the preparatory rites used with the elect on Holy Saturday. In this rite we are invited to open our ears and our mouth "that you may profess the faith you hear to the praise and glory of God."

We are called to be evangelizers! We are called to allow God's Word to live in us, then to live and act in ways that will allow its message to spread to others.

I am conscious of so many people, famous and not so famous, who have worked to bring the healing and reconciling values of Jesus to the many communities they were a part of in this world. Often this occurred at great cost to themselves. People like Anglican Bishop Desmond Tutu of South Africa and Sr. Dorothy Stang, a U. S. missionary in Brazil. Yet there is still so much to do. More effort is needed.

Today's gospel reminds us of our baptismal call to open *our* ears, *our* minds, *our* hearts, to hear the need in our own communities . . . and to respond.

What is it that needs to be "opened" in me to allow me to touch the hearts of those many people thirsting for intimacy and community?

September 13

Twenty-fourth Sunday in Ordinary Time

Monsignor David LeSieur

Lectionary 131B
Mark 8:27-35

Isa 50:4c-9a; Ps 116; Jas 2:14-18

"You are the Christ."

"Who do people say that I am?"

"Who do *you* say that I am?" It's easy to quote public opinion—"Some say this; some say that." But public opinion is never enough for Jesus; he wants to know what *we* think of him.

We agree with Peter: "You are the Christ." But Jesus would ask us what that title means to us. It means Jesus is "God from God, light from light, true God from true God, one in being with the Father." . . . All correct according to creed, but in terms of Mark's gospel a simpler acknowledgment is required. "Christ (Messiah) is the suffering one."

At this point in Mark, Peter's statement that Jesus is the Christ is correct, but it merely scratches the surface of understanding the real identity of "the Christ." When Jesus speaks of his suffering and death, Peter rebukes him, as much as saying that suffering is beneath him. But Jesus will not be swayed from the cross and the pain that goes with it.

Only when we accept the cross as part of Jesus' true identity, and take up our own, will he really know what we think of him.

How has my profession of faith in Jesus the Christ grown and deepened?

September 20

Twenty-fifth Sunday in Ordinary Time

Judy Hoelzeman

Lectionary 134B
Mark 9:30-37

Wis 2:12, 17-20; Ps 54; Jas 3:16–4:3

"Whoever receives one child such as this in my name, receives me."

Today, Jesus asks us to develop the childlike quality of being dependent. That quality comes naturally to infants and children, but not to adults. Jesus' disciples were way off the mark thinking their societal status was important to Jesus.

Most adults fight furiously against becoming dependent. But sometimes they have to give in. Certain illnesses, especially Alzheimer's and other dementia-related illnesses, give them no choice. In the United States, these conditions now affect nearly half of Americans over age eighty-five. Like the child that Jesus gives us as a model today, people with dementia become totally dependent. If we believe today's gospel, these people, whom we often feel so sorry for, may be the greatest servants of all. In these years of childlike dementia, God may very well be working out their salvation, and the salvation of others through them.

Those who care for people with Alzheimer's disease and other dementia-related illnesses also struggle to hold on to control. They want to be "great" and strong as caregivers. But if they are lucky, they soon learn from their loved one to let go and depend on others for help. Then, they too become "great" servants.

What situations are giving me the opportunity to grow more dependent on the Lord and on the help of others?

September 27

Twenty-sixth Sunday in Ordinary Time

Jerre Roberts

Lectionary 137B
Mark 9:38-43, 45, 47-48

Num 11:25-29; Ps 19; Jas 5:1-6

"If your hand causes you to sin, cut it off."

Today's passage from the Gospel of Mark is an example of the symbolic nature of Jesus' teachings. Even the most rigid of fundamentalists would not argue that Jesus ever meant for these words to be taken literally.

But the series of warnings—cutting off one's foot, plucking out one's eye, being thrown into the sea tied to a millstone—illustrates a significant truth. Eliminating sin from one's life calls for drastic measures. Eradicating sin goes deeper than mere superficial behavior. Often it requires painful choices and drastic changes.

While Jesus' words are not to be taken literally, they must be taken seriously. Sin is not simply a problem of behavior, although behavioral change is involved and is necessarily a first step.

Nowadays, the notion of sin seems quaint, a bit outdated, and totally at odds with modern society. Recognizing sinful actions and thoughts in an "anything goes . . . if it feels good do it" environment is difficult.

Sin separates us from God, others, and our truest self. Healing this division restores us to our proper place in God's creation and with renewed strength and energy enables us to live a more authentic life in Christ.

Where do I see the effects of sin in my life and in our world? Am I willing to change with God's help?

October 4

Twenty-seventh Sunday in Ordinary Time

Jerome Kodell, OSB

Lectionary 140B
Mark 10:2-12

Gen 2:18-24; Ps 128; Heb 2:9-11

"And the two shall become one flesh."

In answering the question of the Pharisees about divorce, Jesus quotes the memorable lines of the book of Genesis, "A man shall leave his father and mother and be joined to his wife, and the two shall become one flesh." In Genesis the words are used to describe marital union as a good willed by God in the plan of creation; here Jesus uses them against breaking that union.

We may overlook how countercultural those words are today. Our culture has a wonderful emphasis on the individual rights of each person, but sometimes carries this too far. Marriage is undermined by a spirit of independence which implies that "the two shall remain two." What's mine is mine and what's yours is yours. You give 50 percent and I give 50 percent.

But the divine mandate calls for something sublime: the blending of two mature independent persons into a new one, a new image of God's love in the world. Marriage is a covenant, not a contract, which means it is not for a limited time but forever, and that it doesn't pertain to a part of life but to everything.

Where in life can I give myself 100 percent?

October 11

Twenty-eighth Sunday in Ordinary Time

John Hall

Lectionary 143B
Mark 10:17-30

Wis 7:7-11; Ps 90; Heb 4:12-13

"Good teacher, what must I do to inherit eternal life?"

This gospel reading presents us with the question of following the letter of the law or spirit of the law. Do I drive the speed limit because I don't want to get a ticket? Or is it because I want to be a safe driver and prevent harm to myself and others? For the man in the gospel, the answer would be to avoid a ticket—the letter of the law!

Jesus' reply to the man about his desire to follow God is similar to a teacher responding to a question when a student already knows the answer. Notice that in his response Jesus doesn't mention the first three commandments because these opening commandments hold the answer to the man's question of the key to eternal life. A person can follow the last seven commandments by simply doing what the commandments require, that is, following the letter the law. However, the first three commandments will determine what is in your heart. Clearly, this man's possessions were more important to him than his relationship with God.

What is in my heart?

October 18

Twenty-ninth Sunday in Ordinary Time

Cackie Upchurch

Lectionary 146B
Mark 10:35-45

Isa 53:10-11; Ps 33; Heb 4:14-16

"Whoever wishes to be great among you will be your servant."

Jesus did indeed preach a kingdom that is upside-down and inside-out. The Twelve, those closest to Jesus, must have thought he misspoke when he called them to be servants to one another. They must have scratched their heads and wondered what world he was living in.

The world that Jesus envisioned is a world that transforms power structures so that the least among us benefit the most. It transforms governments so that citizens' needs are more important than institutional survival. It transforms industry so that people and their environment are more important than volume of production. The kingdom Jesus envisioned transforms persons so that greatness can be seen and understood best in the context of simple and humble acts of service.

The kingdom of God has begun in our midst. I recently visited a "great" parish where I could see God's kingdom alive and well. When parishioners became aware that an elderly member of their community was living in dire poverty, they simply pitched in and in a matter of three weeks had gathered materials and built her a new, modest, but safe and cozy home. They explained it simply: "It's what we do. We're Catholics. We're servants."

Where in my life or in my parish do I see signs of service that mark us as members of God's kingdom?

October 25

Thirtieth Sunday in Ordinary Time

Dan Hennessey

Lectionary 149B
Mark 10:46-52

Jer 31:7-9; Ps 126; Heb 5:1-6

"Master, I want to see."

During my residency, to develop empathy for my visually impaired patients, I wore devices that simulated the visual experiences of a person with severe eye disease. I can still recall the helplessness I felt when I was taken out on a busy city sidewalk wearing a device that left me seeing only vague shapes and lights. My guide left me standing there alone. I became disoriented and was afraid to move. It wasn't long before I asked my guide to let me see again.

In this gospel story, Jesus heals the blindness of Bartimaeus. But the miracle in this story is not limited to the restoration of his physical sight. It is a story of the healing of spiritual blindness as well. As followers of Christ, our spiritual blindness disorients and immobilizes us on our spiritual journey. Shedding our spiritual blindness requires us to root out all those things that keep us from following Jesus.

For some, spiritual blindness is rooted in self-centeredness. For others, it lies in the desire to amass more money, power, or possessions. Whatever the cause of our spiritual blindness, we must make the same request of Jesus as Bartimaeus, "Master, I want to see."

When Jesus asks me what I need from him, will I recognize my own need to be healed of spiritual blindness?

November 1

Feast of All Saints

Mary J. Glynn, SJC

Lectionary 667ABC *Rev 7:2-4, 9-14; Ps 24; 1 John 3:1-3*
Matt 5:1-12a

He began to teach them, saying: "Blessed are the poor in spirit . . ."

The walls of Our Lady of the Angels Cathedral in Los Angeles are covered with beautiful tapestries portraying figures of saints from all races and all ages. Eight of these figures among the communion of saints are unnamed and represent those of us striving to live holy lives. The tapestries are a daily reminder that as we listen to Jesus' message he is giving us a blueprint for sainthood.

The beatitudes remind us that we are a kingdom "already, but not yet." In the eyes of the world, poverty, emptiness, sadness, and lack of fame are not desirable options. The gospel turns familiar comforts upside down. The church is a community of people born of the self-giving sacrifice of Christ. The beatitudes remind us that our lives are a blessing only when centered in God's love, the source of kingdom life. They are promptings of the Holy Spirit giving us energy to become the persons God created us to be.

Poverty, hunger, weeping, slander, or even being threatened with death, in whatever forms you or I experience them, is an opportunity to realize and cling to our dependence on God alone. Our challenge is to rejoice and be glad as we continue to strengthen the kingdom among us.

As I pray with the beatitudes, do I hear them as invitations to live in the kingdom of God?

November 8

Thirty-second Sunday in Ordinary Time

Frank Zanoff

Lectionary 155B
Mark 12:38-44

1 Kgs 17:10-16; Ps 146; Heb 9:24-28

"She, from her poverty, has contributed all she had."

In our parishes we have probably had the pastor or a member of the finance council mention the "80-20" rule. Stated simply, they say that 20 percent of the members of our parish contribute 80 percent of the monetary resources needed for our parish to function effectively. Many of us do a quick mental calculation to determine where we stand. The heavy hitters are usually easy to spot. But, is the gift commensurate with blessings received? Do we give always expecting something in return? In our smugness, have we ever tried to pick out the lower tier of givers, being unaware of their personal circumstances? Are we the modern day hypocrites that Mark is describing in this narrative? Just what is our motivation for giving?

The standard for the leaders and well-to-do in Jesus' day was to dress in fine clothing, look pious, and give conspicuously. Like other forms of behavior Jesus observed, this didn't fit in with his message of humility and service in his Father's kingdom. He chastised the scribes and praised the widow. She sacrificed all she had to the temple treasury in her love for God. She, in effect, gave herself.

Where does my giving stop? How can I begin with new fervor to find ways to give of myself?

November 15

Thirty-third Sunday in Ordinary Time

Rosa María Icaza, CCVI

Lectionary 158B
Mark 13:24-32

Dan 12:1-3; Ps 16; Heb 10:11-14, 18

"Heaven and earth will pass away, but my words will not pass away."

Our newspapers, television news programs, and documentary movies seem to give us such a gloomy picture of reality. However, we seldom read or listen to anything that gives us a ray of hope. Today's gospel begins with a similar list of terrible events, but immediately we hear words of light and joy that inspire hope.

As we look around in our world, do we discover God's love and tenderness in a bright sun ray, in a delicate flower, in the singing bird? That is quite easy. But, do we discover God's love even in tragedies of natural disasters? Not long ago, I was conversing with a heart-wise person about this and she said: "Those tragedies are God's urgent call to us to mend our lives and be ready to meet God face to face." God is faithful to his promises of eternal love and mercy. Do we believe them even in the midst of catastrophe and failure?

Our late Holy Father, John Paul II, exhorted us to be messengers of hope. The violent, hateful, and inhuman behavior of some human beings leads us to ask: where is God in all of this? Jesus assures us: "Heaven and earth will pass away, but my words will not pass away." And God is faithful to his promises.

How can I grow in trusting God even when the reality of my world is being turned upside down?

November 22

Feast of Christ the King

Dan Borlik, CM

Lectionary 161B *Dan 7:13-14; Ps 93; Rev 1:5-8*
John 18:33b-37

"My kingdom does not belong to this world . . ."

To this day we struggle with and can misunderstand Jesus' words to Pilate. Maybe a more accurate understanding of this key phrase in this gospel (so say many Scripture scholars) is in this translation of Jesus' answer to Pilate: "My kingdom is *not from* this world . . ." meaning, its source is not from this world.

Pilate and his like even to this day could never conceive of a kingdom without the trappings of power, financial wealth, and probably corruption and violence as well. They most likely think themselves realists. But such "kingdoms" can be little other than products of human imagination and greed.

Jesus, however, as our Lord, is no dreamer—even if what he clearly sees (and asks us to see as well) has its roots in the heavenly Father's plan for creation. For certainly, Jesus' kingdom is for all and for now; it has to do with how we live and act today, and how willingly we suffer the consequences of such a life.

Once we recognize this kingdom, with eyes that see and ears that listen, we are already serving our Lord. The mystery is that then we could not be more free!

How do I imagine Christ's kingdom? Where is my place in that kingdom today?

Contributors

Dan Borlik, CM, is a Vincentian priest currently serving as the provincial of the southern province of his community. He works among Spanish-speaking Catholic immigrants in the areas of sacramental ministry, intercultural communication, and pastoral leadership skills training. He is also a lecturer for Little Rock Scripture Study (LRSS).

Mary J. Glynn, SJC, is a Sister of St. Joseph of Cluny and a native of Galway, Ireland. She has served in a variety of ministries throughout North America and received several degrees from universities in Chicago and Canada. She is the current director of religious education and Christian initiation for the Diocese of Little Rock and coordinates the diocesan Theology Institute.

Roy Goetz, a deacon in Subiaco, Arkansas, is a skilled musician who teaches New Testament Scriptures and is the director of instrumental music at Subiaco Academy, where he is also campus minister.

John Hall holds a master's degree in pastoral studies, has served in a number of pastoral positions for the Diocese of Little Rock, is a current member of the LRSS board of directors, and appears as a lecturer on recorded materials. His position as a property manager and real estate agent keeps him in touch with the marketplace.

Msgr. J. Gaston Hebert served as the Administrator of the Diocese of Little Rock from June 2006 to June 2008. A former classroom teacher and pastor, he is an effective preacher and writer.

Dan Hennessey is a deacon serving in a downtown Little Rock parish and a frequent lecturer for LRSS. He is a doctor of optometry in full-time practice.

Lilly Hess is an associate director for Little Rock Scripture Study and has worked with this ministry for most of its thirty-five years. Among her duties she is responsible for the production of all recorded materials. She works closely with the finance department of Liturgical Press as well.

Judy Hoelzeman holds a master's of religious education and is a frequent lecturer for LRSS. She is married and has worked largely with education and advocacy for the elderly and those who are caregivers for the aging. She currently is volunteer coordinator with a hospice in Little Rock, Arkansas.

Rosa María Icaza, CCVI, is professor emerita of foreign languages at the University of the Incarnate Word, and associate director of the programs department at the Mexican American Cultural Center, both located in San Antonio, Texas. She has been a primary translator for LRSS materials since our Spanish materials were introduced.

Jerome Kodell, OSB, the Abbot of Subiaco Abbey in Arkansas, is a retreat director, Scripture scholar, and writer. He authored all of the original study materials for LRSS and has remained a valued advisor to this ministry.

Msgr. David LeSieur is pastor of St. Vincent de Paul Catholic Church in Rogers, Arkansas, and is director of continuing formation for clergy for the Diocese of Little Rock. He is a frequent lecturer for LRSS and has served on its board of directors.

Susan McCarthy, RDC, is the workshop and promotion coordinator for LRSS. Much of her previous work has been in teaching and pastoral ministry in the Archdiocese of New York, where she also earned her master's in pastoral ministry. She can be seen on a number of recorded wrap-up lectures.

Robert L. Morris is actively involved in all kinds of community and parish ministry as a deacon in Heber Springs, Arkansas. He and his wife, Marie, served as staff members for diaconate formation in the Diocese of Little Rock and have been actively involved in LRSS for a number of years.

Marie Morris is a vital member of her parish and actively involved in a number of parish and community ministries. She and her husband, Robert, have served in leadership with the Subiaco Abbey Coury House retreat league.

Jerre Roberts is often seen or heard on LRSS taped materials. As a professional storyteller of sacred stories for the past twenty years and former director of adult formation and

RCIA, she has directed retreats and workshops on sacred stories throughout the country.

Cackie Upchurch is the director of LRSS and has authored study guides and wrap-up lectures. She serves as an associate editor for *The Bible Today* and has presented workshops and retreat days around the country. Cackie earned two degrees in theology and is involved in a variety of adult faith formation efforts in the Diocese of Little Rock.

Nancy Lee Walters serves as the customer service representative for the Scripture Study office in Little Rock. In her twenty-two years with LRSS she has helped direct numerous people to the materials they need. She and her husband, Tony, are active members of their parish in Little Rock.

Macrina Wiederkehr, OSB, author and spiritual guide, is a Benedictine of St. Scholastica Monastery in Arkansas. Her books include *The Song of the Seed* and *Gold in Your Memories*. Her most recent book is *Seven Sacred Pauses: Living Mindfully Through the Hours*. She also writes "Romancing the Word" in *Stepping Stones*, the online newsletter of LRSS. Macrina is a popular retreat director throughout North America. See www.MacrinaWiederkehr.com

Gregory C. Wolfe is director of finance for the Diocese of Little Rock. In addition to an MBA, he also holds a bachelor's degree in theology and a master's in formative foundational spirituality and has been a frequent lecturer for Bible study.

Greg was also the first president of the LRSS board of directors.

Clifford M. Yeary holds a master's degree in pastoral studies and a bachelor's degree in Old Testament literature. Among his duties as Associate Director of LRSS, he is responsible for writing and revising study materials, and presenting wrap-up lectures. Cliff is the author of the online LRSS series, *What the Bible Says About . . .*, as well as a number of study guides.

Frank Zanoff, a deacon in Fairfield Bay, Arkansas, is the current president of the board of directors for LRSS and a longtime coordinator of Bible study in his parish. He is immersed in parish activities and in community outreach with his wife, Gail.

About Little Rock Scripture Study

Little Rock Scripture Study began in 1974 by developing materials that could be used in small groups by people interested in Bible study in Catholic parishes. In the past thirty years, over three million study sets have been used by participants all over North America and in over 50 countries beyond its borders.

The method of Little Rock Scripture Study involves daily prayer and study, weekly small group prayer and faith sharing, accompanied by a weekly wrap-up lecture. The purpose is not simply to acquire knowledge, though biblical literacy is one good result. The more important focus of Bible study is to grow in relationship with God and with the believing community.

Little Rock Scripture Study is a ministry of the Diocese of Little Rock in Arkansas in partnership with Liturgical Press in Collegeville, Minnesota. The staff in Little Rock develops the study materials, produces the taped materials, presents diocesan workshops, organizes a yearly summer Bible Institute, and puts together the newsletter *Stepping Stones,* which is published three times each year. Liturgical Press edits and publishes the study materials, designs marketing pieces, maintains the website, and oversees all orders and shipping.

For more information about Little Rock Scripture Study and the materials available for group study, contact:

Little Rock Scripture Study
2500 North Tyler Street
Little Rock, AR 72207

Phone: 501-664-0340 in Arkansas or
800-858-5434 in Minnesota

e-mail: lrss@dolr.org

website: www.littlerockscipture.org